The Forest Under the Sea

JOHN BARNIE

Published by Cinnamon Press
Meirion House
Glan yr afon
Tanygrisiau
Blaenau Ffestiniog
Gwynedd
LL41 3SU
www.cinnamonpress.com

The right of John Barnie to be identified as author of this work has been asserted by him in accordance with the Copyright, Designs and Patent Act, 1988. Copyright © 2010 John Barnie
ISBN: 978-1-907090-04-2
British Library Cataloguing in Publication Data. A CIP record for this book can be obtained from the British Library.

All rights reserved. No part of this publication may be reproduced, stored in a retrieval system, or transmitted in any form or by any means, electronic, mechanical, photocopying, recording or otherwise without either the prior written permission of the publishers. This book may not be lent, hired out, resold or otherwise disposed of by way of trade in any form of binding or cover other than that in which it is published, without the prior consent of the publishers.

Designed and typeset in Palatino by Cinnamon Press. Cover design by Mike Fortune-Wood from original artwork 'Petrified Forest' by George Burba.
Printed in Great Britain by the MPG Books Group,
Bodmin and King's Lynn.

Cinnamon Press is represented in the UK by Inpress Ltd www.inpressbooks.co.uk and in Wales by the Welsh Books Council www.cllc.org.uk.

The publisher acknowledges the financial assistance of the Welsh Books Council.

Acknowledgements

Some of these poems first appeared in *English*, *Poetry Salzburg*, *Poetry Wales*, and *Staple*.

'The Game of Love' contains a slightly modified quotation ('jack of diamonds, jack of / diamonds, a hard card to play') from Blind Lemon Jefferson, *Jack O'Diamond Blues* (1926).

My thanks to Helle Michelsen for her criticism.

And a note

Cantre'r Gwaelod ('The Lowland Hundred'), an area of land which, as the last Ice Age ended, stretched fourteen miles to the West in what is now Cardigan Bay. Legends about the Cantref and its inhabitants reach back to the Mesolithic when the area was inundated by rising sea levels.

At Borth, Clarach and Tany-y-bwlch stumps and sometimes toppled trunks of Scots pine and oak are revealed at low tide. They are the outer edge of the Forest Under the Sea, all that is visible of Cantre'r Gwaelod.

Contents

Big Bend Country	9
Spider Crabs	10
Atlantic Trawler	11
Razor Shells at Ynys las	12
Nature	13
The Asset Strippers	14
Too Late Then	15
Understanding Nature	16
In a Field Near Abergavenny	17
Little Egret	18
Long-Tailed Tits in Winter	19
Gwdihŵ	20
The Walnut Tree	21
The Hunter Explains	22
The Shoot	23
You Have to Be Flexible	24
How Do You Say 'Hello'?	25
At the Drowned Forest	26
Low Tide at Borth	27
A Rider at Ynys Las	28
Yesterday is a Long Time Ago	29
Borth	30
Cantre'r Gwaelod	31
Happy Birthday	32
How it Was	33
The Hyacinths of Norman Place	34
White Castle	35
Seeing Myself	36
Barry Island	37
Summer's Ending	38
Bus Conducting on the Western Welsh	39

Topkapi Sarayi	40
The Digitoi	41
Open to the Public	42
The Game of Love	43
Punctuated Equilibrium	44
No Going Back	45
Scene from a Film Noir	46
Day Number One	47
A Guest in This Life	48
Getting By	49
An Afternoon	50
Are You Quite Sure?	51
What She Said	52
Couldn't Say	53
Post Operational	54
Or is it a Schottische?	55
Circus	56
The Image	57
Today	58
Deus Absconditus	59
A Shopkeeper's View of the Universe	60
The Periodicity of Comets	61
At St Mary's	62
Rosemary	63
A Jar of Honey	64

In our activity alone do we find the sustaining illusion of an independent existence as against the whole scheme of things of which we form a helpless part.
                    Joseph Conrad, *Nostromo*

The Forest Under the Sea

Big Bend Country

Play me something riverine
about eels, the fistful of cables
slipping from the engineer's
hands, rubberised against the shock of the
charge that sends them quivering
upstream to enter every orifice
of a sheep snagged by its woolly
jumper on an alder, the roomy
skull and ribcage a shanty home
for a while; you don't knock there
for a welcome from eyes that see only
prey, from jaws that can only snap
shut on life; let's tiptoe away
to admire the glitter of the shallows
where the old ferry used to be,
hauled on a steel rope from bank to
bank like a weary shuttle.

Spider Crabs

If I can climb
over the backs of my brothers and sisters
to the hands manhandling this cage

I'll tear them to red confetti
for a blood wedding;

pity is a word thrown overboard by Noah;
It tasted good,

said the lips of the shark.

Atlantic Trawler

The net bulging with fish
released in a rubbery fall to the deck

where the gutting starts and innards are flung
over the running roof of the sea

to gulls' screams and the alighting of webbed feet;
what were the faces doing at the net's windows mouthing O O O;

too late to get a handle on the air
when they're packed in ice and boxed,

when their sequins silver the tarmac
and they're driven away.

Razor Shells at Ynys Las

Hundreds of barbers here
for a convention except
they've abandoned their blades, as if
they remembered the moon's eye

sliced through in that
film and couldn't go
on, leaving the sand to be
clean shaved by the tide.

Nature

Thick-flighted fulmars,
and kittiwakes in migraine patterns over a seine-net,
as two men haul on the oars;

an owl's cry down the long drift of the night,
and the hungry stars
eating at the edge of our thoughts.

The Asset Strippers

Crows are tool users, did you
know; with AK-47s
they'd gun down the world; checks, checks,
and balances; how did we pick the locks

and escape (there was much discussion
in the boardroom of the gods); *Pan
troglodytes* has had its day,
fishing for termites with a stick.

Too Late Then

In the last days of Europe
I saw a dipper on a mountain stream
and a tank crushing gorse and bracken
as it plunged down a slope through

fences and dry-stone walls; the
dipper was infuriating, it seemed so free
from everything except the river that
bound it with swift ropes of water.

Understanding Nature

Your move,
the beetle said,
clinging to my sweater
in leafy browns;

What game are we
playing; Any
game you like;
I picked it off

and threw it through the
window; *Check*, I
shouted; the beetle
shouted *Mate*.

In a Field Near Abergavenny

What do I know,
answered the crow,
The sky is no door,
the earth is no grave,

there is no path
leading out of the world;
the crow twirled,
its companions too,

hanging from twine
under an oak,
released for ever
from the mirrors and smoke.

Little Egret

Citrus yellow feet, plonk, plonk,
these are the property of *me*,

and governor-general's cockatoo plumes
blowing in an on-shore wind;

if I see a shrimp with its engine running
in a pool left behind by the tide,

a jerk of the head and I
beak it; nothing passes me by.

Long-tailed Tits in Winter

Long-tailed tits
turned out for a wedding,
all bridal bows and
bouquets, threading bare
twigs in the lane; some

hang upside down
on black-water boughs
then chase off, ribbons
flowing, disowning everything
if paradise is not here.

Gwdihŵ

My name is gwdihŵ
and my home is Wales, I
have never flown to England
though I hear gwdihŵs
there saying Come over the silver
stream to our woods where
the catching is excellent; they
use such hungry words
like ladders to the Moon;
why would I leave Wales,
its lonelinesses; we
have silver streams too
where the English draw up
covered waggons; but again
I fly away, a feather
shadow; gwdihŵ, gwdihŵ.

The Walnut Tree

That's it, the disassembled
trunk a fallen emperor's column,
the parked canopy a wig for

Fuzzy the Clown; rot was the thief
climbing through the wood, giving Death
a leg-up; goldfinches alighted there

last week, so chattery, when the tree
was still a bird-cage
carried in the jumpy hand of the wind.

The Hunter Explains

Being human is the trigger;
yes, I shoot woodcock, grey lag, too,
wood pigeons with red-muscled breasts;

(let's have a feather-
plucking in the shed, and a
hunter's stew;)

so come on, little birds,
while stiff-fingered cartridges
poke me in the ribs

I'll tread the edge of your world
with Mr Nosey's black nostrils,
smelling of gun-oil and death.

The Shoot

When a pheasant falls
from the top to the bottom of its
world, tumbling over winter
stubble, the cartridge is expressed

from the breech like a tabloid
blonde, glossed lips mouthing *Mmwhaa*
to fingers that cast it
without thought in the mud.

You Have to be Flexible

The knife cuts at the sheep's
lungs that resist pillow-wise
with a wheezy breath; the lungs
awry on the chopping board, the
cat following my hand with its
eyes; it'll eat the chunks cheek-on,
grinding the shiny-foam breathing
aparatus the sheep used to
negotiate its field; oxygen, lungs,
blood, the simple exchange; I
slip the slippery pink pieces onto a
plate and the cat sidles up.

How do you say 'Hello'?

There's no entry in *The Rough Guide to Cantre'r Gwaelod*
under Language,

as you stand at the drowned forest's edge
where a herring gull shuffles its feathers;

a sentimentalist would throw a wreath of words from a boat
                                                two miles out
for the dogfish and the mackerel;

six thousand years ago, girls
dunking buckets in the streams

would run from the words
and the gates would be closed;

there are no words to send to the Cantref;
each chain of words comes back broken from the sea.

At the Drowned Forest

Perhaps when it's over
a poem from a house or library
will bowl along in the wind,
to be slapped on a stump

whose roots emerge with the tide,
now there, now here;
for today, the wet sands at Ynys Las

(Borth obscured by rain)
are a long empty boulevard stretching away
where there's no one to tip a hat to
in the human promenade.

Low Tide at Borth

Terns have settled for a chat
at ease among roots of the sunken forest
like woodland birds before the tide
turns to reclaim its property, wrapping it
in salty preservatives; the terns

will fly, then, and screech and dive
for the silver mint of fish, the shoal
scattering and shining as did leaves in the Cantref
when a westerly blew and there was fierce
gale-light and no mercy.

A Rider at Ynys Las

A girl and a horse
travel the tide-line, side-
stepping wavelets; I'd

say they were tip-toeing but
each deep indent in the
sand leaves a mirror

the breadth of a face,
for me to see how the sky
teeters in blue.

Yesterday is a Long Time Ago

Those learned doctors, the
crabs, have failed to find
a single word carved on bark
for them to read with incinerator

eyes, and the sea has given up
on the leaves of Cantre'r
Gwaelod that never rustle
in the waterwinds of the currents.

Borth

From the perspective of the
inhabitants, Borth has
always been there with the sea's

breathing the other side of the wall,
and balsa wood fleets of gulls
at high tide; at low,

the drowned forest of the
Cantref, oak and pine, steps out
of the sand

with a different assemblage of facts,
that don't add up to the
long street and the bus

dwindling between parallel
lines to Ynys Las where,
for now, the story ends.

Cantre'r Gwaelod

I'm trying to recall the wreckage of my parents' lives,
my brother's,

confounded with claws and tree stumps on the shore
as

memory sweeps their images
out and in.

Happy Birthday

My darling boring perambulator where I sit with a bland face
while it's flounced round the park

and a tree creeper skips up a copper beech;

it's sunny and spring
and although on the hills bracken is criss-crossed in death

there's going to be a resurrection, a kerfuffle of baby greens;

later an inspection party of grouse
and a raven doing a victory roll;

what's my part in this in the big brown pram;

useless to ask my mother who's so proud;
it's the beginning of the world; nineteen-forty-one.

How it Was

Chrome was too posh, mouthing
its O and judicious Mmmm, too
much the shopkeeper's favourite
kettle and electric toaster, in the Fifties;

did she wear a pillbox hat, did she
wear high heels and a skirt with
layers of petticoats; chrome

had answers with a faceful of
shine, breathed on and polished,
pretending to show the wobbly
reflection of ourselves, when really it

bent the sun in a master-stroke,
around its shoulders in a shawl
of calculated light.

The Hyacinths of Norman Place

Little buddhas on thrones of earth
intoning the great Om
in the darkness of a cupboard

while outside wind and rain
give the World a lashing; wait
till they breed shoots of coolness

clammy to the touch
in pots of terracotta, then
move them to windowsills;

as they green they become girls,
dumpy, perhaps, and the party frocks
all wrong, and those eighteenth-century perms,

someone should have told them; Still,
they say, when you see us dancing by ourselves
don't call us wallflowers;

we're the sign of winter's Untergang
and of springtime rising
like a face in the lake

where they believed it had drowned.

White Castle

Cycling from town was best
paying at the wooden booth
the colour of wasps' nests,

not come for history's
ground-plan as the castle's shadow
yawned and stretched,

and hedgerows where yellowhammers
bred, channelled slow tarmac
streams down lanes; time told

on the cow parsleys' dials
where flies alighted
in a flicker of silence.

Seeing Myself

The dentist and his nurse press against the wall
in a B-movie horror poster
while the evil beam clicks through my cheek,

walk back nonchalantly
to examine the death-print of my jaw;

Wiggle your toes,
and I did in the Fifties' shop,

my bones never more alive than when I watched them dance
in the green light of the machine;

A check-up in six months; that's fine;
I do the graveyard strut down Terrace Road.

Barry Island

The deckchair looks like it'll
give you a bad back, its striped
canvas part of an old-fashioned
gaiety now, that you eased into
with a sigh while the sea glitter
and sky-blue-blindness made you
close your eyes, overwhelmed with
shrieks and gull calls, the plush
slap of wavelets and their retreat,
as the ocean's breath played out
on the beach; brightness for ever;
but the chairs are clapper-boarded
together, left in attics and sheds where
the fabric fades and rots quietly
as if the past were talking to itself.

Summer's Ending

When I was a child
Death called at other people's
houses and sometimes the curtains
were drawn and a hearse climbed slowly
up Hereford Road; now,

he sits in a deckchair on my lawn
leafing through *The Plumed Serpent*, saying,
I can't get on with this at all; glancing
at the windows in that lazy summer way
if he catches a movement; what time is it;
oh late; the swifts have wiped the blue
                      slate of the
                            sky

clean.

Bus Conducting on the Western Welsh

Abergavenny to Brecon, 1960

The sun stood back from the eastern hills
as our shadow leapt along hedgerows
and gates; passengers

got on at Bwlch
but never at Scethrog; at Brecon
bacon sandwiches and tea;

could there be humans on the Moon;
Charlie O'Brien thought so; pockets of air, see,
or underground;

faces of passengers were familiar
and strange as Yucatán
stepping up into the maroon bus and stepping off;

at Crickhowell the Table Mountain
spread for summer, with wheatears
and larks;

my Hundred of the Deeps
where all are drowned
and I can neither swim nor breathe.

Topkapi Sarayi

The boredom of grandeur
is a new thought, not
in the guide books yet; a

throne of gold, a hilt,
dutifully sparkling with
jewels; dull as our ghost-

impressions in the glass;
through the Bosphorus
warships glide, grey swans

fuelled by oil,
sailing to their nests
in Black Sea ports.

The Digitoi

Santa Sofia, Istanbul

What are the digitoi doing
arms outstretched in a new form of
ecstatic prayer, fingers

clasped round a tiny bright screen
shuffling beneath God's dome
and its scaffolding;

everyone here speaks Babelonic,
a trodden murmur of
syllables; not Saint Peter

but the ticket seller, bored
at the gate; Santa Sofia where
is your wisdom and your crown?

Open to the Public

The grand ladies of Europe
painted in oils; Louise, Louise,
famous for her necklines and a soft

mouth; was history no more than a
brush stroke, no more than light
caught by the artist in a glittering

eye; at night the sky is full of stars
calling each other's names across
space, lonely as whales.

The Game of Love

Do you feel inhibited by love
setting its cards out quietly
on the baize; jack of diamonds, jack of
diamonds, a hard card to play; the
croupier watches, ready with his rake,
there's a hush in the room and the
lights are dimmed; someone calls the
manager; if you walk out with empty
hands, there's always the dawn or a crest-
fallen church announcing its services,
the tea shack starting up with lights
and egg baps; even the sea is
still there, rattling the pebbles awake
in its restless cradle.

Punctuated Equilibrium

The poor of the world
squatting before a
question mark, before
an exclamation mark,
before a full stop.

No Going Back

There's the statue to the Dignity of Man
toppled over and a hand pointing up through
brambles, and the rotting watchtower with its tannoy'd
voice singing, *I did it my way*; toadstools

push their heads through needles on the forest floor
like folk tales jumped out of the books;
so there *was* something to it, though we'll never find
the witch and the gingerbread house now.

Scene from a Film Noir

Fishing from the city's reefs,
playing for big ones in the murky down-below wrecks;

did we build much, did we have hopes;
all the questions that were piled in backyard skips

and driven through the night streets to the prams
that sailed to open water and dropped them in anoxic deeps.

Day Number One

We need heavy duty pressure gauges for this life,
a good block and tackle to send a man down

singing *Free as a bird, bird, bird,*
free as a bird;

John the Baptist lost his head,
Jesus thought a gravestone was a door;

at Yad Vashem it's the lizards are most alive
downloading energy from the Sun,

not the crowds of recruits with their casually slung guns
lectured on death, that game of tag

from darkness to light
and into darkness again.

A Guest in this Life

The presents in the drawer,
but where is the hand that wrapped them;

the footfall of the postman
and his shadow against the glass;

the phone in the hall with its receiver of questions;
bird cheep and traffic drone;

time is only the great clock of the Sun
dragging its light across floors;

I want you, I need you,
from the radio next door;

seek meaning if you like but it's gone,
her clothes untouched, the electric cooker turned off;

last bills in the hall
attributed to her name.

Getting By

Just a foothold out of this bin of bones,
that's what the Christians pray;

just a hand from God
for that beautiful girl over there;

She's dying, the parents moan;

the other great apes don't see
Death's shadow spread out on the concrete,

so they sit in their cages all day
with moist eyes

that swim, almost, with personality.

An Afternoon

Let the grandmothers
wheel the prams, let them be
bossy; Death waits,

hat tipped over the empty sockets
of his eyes, leaning against the door-
frame where the rippling shadows of
swifts measure the time.

Are You Quite Sure?

The Church of John the Baptist
is a blue-tiled stove turned outside in,
cold after sunlight splashing off streets and walls;

religious tourists and parties of schoolgirls
roam about,

and there, bending, there
is the cave where the old nut was born,
rough like an oyster shell,

unspeakable Earth leering out at our feet;

no wonder they have big candles waving in prayer's breath,
hoping the Baptist will intercede,
touching Jesus' sleeve.

What She Said

The girl who'd been shot through the head
and left for dead had a third eye;

What's it like, asked her friends;

A red curtained window in an attic
and blood splashed over boxes of apples;
if I stand on tiptoe I think I can see,

but always the obstinate red
and a sun shining through flesh;

Would you rather *be* dead;

No, I like it here with the smell of apples;
the must of them easing to waxy decay
as winter darkens.

Couldn't Say

Who owns the body?
I do, says the mind, from my room with twin windows;

but it doesn't like to think
how the brain's porridge can be splashed on walls,

how the corpse in the coffin is thinking nothing at all,
eyes inward above cool grey hands;

Here is the cerebellum, says the anatomist,
with its crocodile darkness;

and what about dreams bubbling through the floors;

the body rouses,
Let's have a drink, my troubled friend.

Post Operational

Nothing can bring back the
ghost breast which she
feels at night suckling the
child, a Madonna of one
possibility lost among wildly
reproducing cells, and che-
micals sipped by the blood
to kill and be kind to the once
beautiful body, returning her to
normality as dawn opens a
grey morning on its stealthy
hinges, and looks in.

Or is it a Schottische?

It's natural to back away
when he offers his hand,
and as I'll explain, I'm no
dancing man myself,

but the orchestra's tuned,
and violins rattle under
bony chins as the maestro
looks up; Iwan the farmer, I

recognise him, and Olive
drws nesaf, all suitably attired
in the rags of their lives
for the last, slow, pavane.

Circus

The snarl of the old
as Death, their trainer,
backs them against the bars,
no chair upended, no showy whip,
no moustache or top hat,

just the jawbone's ancient laugh
and the stare through the blue
to the darkness beyond.

The Image

For them it wasn't quaint
it was fashion, and the photograph
took a section through the living
flesh; don't forget,

time buries us all in its
waste tips, the JCBs working
night and day, bulling up to a roar
to topple the present

into the past.

Today

We hold the human
bowl out to the stars but it's
a poor catcher of answers; what
gods there were are dissolved
in sea mist or drops of dew, even
Jesus works as a hospital night
porter trundling bags of linen to be
washed; nobody's sure how to spell
prophet any longer, confusing it with
jackpots and the knowing crooked
smile of the blonde girl in the ads.

Deus Absconditus

They've dusted for fingerprints,
swabbed for DNA, dug up graves
where the lettering is worn;
murder, or suicide; He's here,

say the Catholics, Or there,
say the Calvinists; everywhere
and nowhere, torn on a paradox;

let's go out in the lanes
to the season's last butterflies,
gatekeepers holding luminous
browns ajar in their wings.

A Shopkeeper's View of the Universe

November roses
crowd the panes, a gift
I planted to myself,

while cloud is hauled across the sky
like a tailor measuring time,
grey and endless,

until the universal clock strikes 12
and an unknown hand
turns the sign to *Closed*.

The Periodicity of Comets

There it is, a ploughman driving a furrow through space,
sheering light from the blade as it heads for the Sun;

below on Earth pale Jesus hangs from the cross small as a mouse
and Judas hangs quietly from an olive tree;

sunbirds and bulbuls begin another day in the Valley of Gehenna;

the ploughman ploughs on;

nothing is planted in the black furrow,
and no one is at the curtain of time wondering what to do.

At St Mary's

Funerals give us the gift
of emptiness; can you catch sunlight,
can you eat shadow;

the hymns are ladders of water,
the oration an address to statues
lost in the blue Pacific

of their own mortality.

Rosemary

Do you remember me, she
asked as mourners backed up,
like cautious sheep at a gap
in the fence; we shook hands
and I noticed she had the same
kind eyes; the mourners were
patient, then one stepped out
of the shadow's pen as she
walked away among flowers
in the spring's harsh light.

A Jar of Honey

When Ra's tears fell to
Earth they became bees, every-
one knows that, fanning
out among glades and into
the throats of flowers; evo-
lution was saved, as a temple-
priest might say, nodding wisely
to the biologist; but why

was a hawk-god crying, out there,
in the cold acres of space;
was it the man trying to tear off
the bird's face, unable to bear
the rictus any longer; were the
bees a message that was mis-
understood as the first men scraped
honey from hives in the ur-wood.